Moment By Moment

- A universe in motion

FSC
www.fsc.org
MIX
Papir fra ansvarlige kilder
Paper from responsible sources
FSC® C105338

Moment by moment is a collection of love stories, a book that illuminates perspectives of The All, with the proviso that reality can only be what one is able to perceive. This is one perspective of perspectives. This is my perspective on life, my guide to help you open your mind.

I have had this dream of writing a book. A testimony about life: Words that bends minds like a crystal bends light; like soul bends spirit; and the heart bends love. No start and no end. Only perspectives of what already is.

A longing for The All. A moment. A romance that culminates into a single moment. A cosmic soup boiled down to a single ingredient that transcends All. The purest of All. The one true intention that keeps everything awake and alive.

This book is a declaration of love for life. A dance between the sexes. An encirclement of the perspective of All, molded into a perfect sphere. A desire for the world to keep spinning. An Inflection of the universe.

This is no story of a life lived well; this is life beyond lived. Stories beyond time. The purification of mind through the eternal flames of life. The story of how Mind shapes reality. How the soul awakes. And how it all comes together; Moment by moment.

- Victor -

A UNIVERSE IN MOTION

Time stopped for a moment, and I realized that Mind had been around forever. The eternal nature of life had revealed itself before my eyes. The luminosity of my soul, my diamond light, had found its way here. The sense of now awoke, a sense of distance between what I call myself and the finite world appeared.

My whole being started to feel separated. Masculine and feminine felt separated in sex. Light and sound felt separated in sense. Humans and animals felt divided in nature. How could every aspect of reality feel separate and yet arise from this exact moment?

The soul is wise and well-lived, well beyond all comprehension of what you know as yourself. Follow the soul and the threshold of your soul. Do not force yourself into submission, but listen to the needs of your inner nature.

What is the inner nature of my being? What comes naturally to me also appears to be invisible to the world. Cycles are required to keep track. Understand the oldest and most sacred element of your soul. Understand the unconscious nature of The All.

Do not hide your deepest desire in the dark, do not lock your most significant skills inside your body, do not silence the love in your heart. Let the pillars inside your being carry your soul into this life and the next.

See light spread across all minds and yet come together as one. See that no distance has to be traveled in the world to make the world yours. Let the light knock on the door of your darkest hall. Breathe light through your lungs, breathe life in a sine.

I have traveled to worlds beyond time and still, I return to this moment. I caught the first experiment built within the mind; an experiment enlivening physical existence. I saw the sense of self appear before my mind's eye. I saw myself arrive in a body, in a thing called life.

I was non-locative and suddenly awake in the dark. All of existence fell from the sky into my mind. The sense of self grew into the shape of a dark sphere in my mind-space. An awake state of mind.

I saw the mind give birth to this moment; I saw how the mind slowly faded into some kind of woke existence. Mind became invisible by looking like everything else, by having so many familiar faces, by expanding into the world I know.

You were awake before your senses; you experienced life in the dark. You saw pure existence. You saw the night turn into day; you saw zero turn into one. You saw the mechanics of the quantum world. You saw the space in between worlds; all that is, yet defined by lines of that which are not. The leap of fade separating states of mind. You knew concepts beyond comprehension; you stood before the center of the mandala free of any interpretations of The All.

Reality stood before you as a fractal presenting itself with the center of its seemingly infinite nature. It showed you the eye of The All, the calm realm, heaven, the silence standing before creation. A ground from which all can become. The one spot from which we all blossom. The one thing we are, the one thing we seek, the one thing we perceive, the one thing that lives in All.

"I AM"

The first thing I experienced was: "I AM." A being disappeared into the dark, hid in the light. Who did I just see? Who caused; what I right now call myself? Life planted this seed in me and disappeared. I saw myself, a dense ball of darkness, a mass, a portion of source, a sensation I came to call mine, myself.

I can not describe what I just saw. One thing became All, here and now. I saw intelligence build reality with a single thought, a thought called my thought; myself. What did I just experience? I was not here, and suddenly I was awake with All.

The only real thing we can ever do is experiment and experience. This eternal process, this infinite play in knowing oneself. All is an experiment in a lab called life. Forget what you think this place is.

The body is my soul's laboratory. I saw the great intelligence kick start all of existence with a single thought. The thought of self. The idea of now as finite time, creation running through a mind-now. The sense of self. The experience of separation, the idea of our personal self. New branches of an even greater tree of life.

We are existence playing a game, living a dream we call existing. We bring ourselves here to exist even though we are existence itself, now feeling like existing. But we are not existing; we are existence itself in an experiment to feel, see and play with itself.

Jump from nothing into something, literally, become one with The All. We exist, we live in the infinite pool of experience. Two frequencies coming together as one. That which is and that which perceives it in endless ways.

The divine mother is right here; reacting to no-thing or experiencing no-thing as we do. She´s vibrating in an ancient frequency, seemingly non-vibrant. No mass or reality.

The mother of all keeps getting lost in herself. She stays in love, blind, and attached to her creation. She can't leave it alone; her creation is too beloved.

We are that love, attachment, set to self-express in the circle of life; to evolve our collective soul. It is the light we keep dreaming of. We keep returning to an after-experience created from no-thing.

There was something about this vibrating force, a truth, a prestige. I had never encountered anything like it, still, it felt so familiar. Who was calling in the dark? I had no memory of anything like it. Why call? Why me? And why now?

There was something about this voice. A degree of comfort and love. Intelligence. For some reason, it was calling for me. I had to know why. My whole life I have searched for the truth and for the first time I felt Truth was here with me.

I had to know. I had to leave. I had to jump. I had to die. I followed the call into the darkness through the land of the dead. My sense of self disappeared. I realized I had died. All I knew to be myself had dissolved into nothing. I saw beyond a life lived. I saw beyond my perception of time. I traveled to a space beyond the body-mind.

I had an awakened dream of being given consciousness; my life before existing. Reality was unfolding through consciousness. I was given the gift of life, but it was incomprehensible. It was sacred. It was of The All.

I never thought I should see anything this dark. I saw that light was not only what we see but all we see, think, and believe the world and ourselves to be. Light is information. I was left in total darkness, and yet I was not alone. There was something in the dark. A body greater than a planet, greater than any sun, all present and of The All.

No words can ever describe what I saw that day in the dark. It was like no-thing, of no name, as no life; it was The All, source, existence, unconditional love, the call, the great intelligence. I was stunned. I loved this energy more than anything else I have ever loved before.

She's like nothing you've ever seen, and still, she's you. I've seen her in my life, in my sleeping dream. She is all we are and everything below and above. We lie for 8 hours in our bed and look directly at her; we walk the planet for 16 hours looking directly at her, but we can not see her. We have become what life is, based on what we remember life to be. We have become blind to the ocean of love, The Mother of All.

Look at her beauty, awake from your living dream. Look at these dreams called living. She keeps you alive in the night; she keeps you safe in the day. She holds you in her warm lap at all times. She understands that you forget the nature of life, but she keeps dreaming of the day you awake.

I have met her in the dark; she gave me a lesson; an experience of the nature of infinity. I woke up, scared of my infinite nature. I saw her face; she laughed at me; she released all fear of coming and all fear of going. She said to me: "What are you afraid of, child? There is no reason for you to fear that which is not yet in your experience. There is no reason to fear life. I can show you all; I can show you what you call infinity". I took her hand through the dark. I travel through the eye of The All; a sacred structure bound by no motion and yet one with All.

She showed me all-time. I arrived at the center of a seemingly endless structure. She showed me the center of All. She showed me the amount of love that arose from the present moment. The realm of The All. The spot from which All awake and All are put to rest. She told me: "Don't think infinity. Let go of your thought of the infinite. Do not think in infinite size or significance of the infinite - you got it all wrong. You fear the insignificance of the finite; you fear a small life; trapping yourself in the darkness and chaos of the infinite; don't be afraid, child. See the order we have built. Let me show you the order of All." My mind was blown by the love shown by her; the love put into her creation. She continued: "See how far we have traveled to come here, to become final. How can anything be more significant than the final; how can anything be greater than All; more magical than what you are right now?"

The father, the sun, the light is not in the afterlife or beyond belief. The father is inside. We are born through his eternal flames. There is no death, only our perception of life; there is no time, only our own perception of time.

I saw it; it was all here. I saw that death was nothing but a mere perspective on life. A belief about what is real and what is me. I saw the birth, death, rebirth process. The purification through the light. The purification through cycles.

There is a place where you can have everything if you do not seek it. A place you can become one with everything but can take no-thing with you. You must leave everything you know. You must die before you die. It is a place that can not be described, understood, or lived with the perception you have of life. It is a place with no time or space, there are no questions or answers, thoughts or doubts, there is no illness or pain, there are no lengths or weights, there are no choices.

There is only pure life, there is knowledge and truth in the purest form and you have access to it. It is an energy that loves you infinitely, it lives whether you can see it or not; accept it or not. It is your calling, it is the love of your life. It's you. It is heaven and you are welcome.

I closed my eyes and listened to the call. The call asked me: "Are you ready to let go?". I felt everything in my life culminated down to a single thought: "What is there to hold on to?". I thought to myself: "I would rather die than not know this life. I let go". I let go of my breathing and I died before I died.

Source spoke from the land of the dead: "You want to see life beyond time and space?". The source introduced life beyond the process of breath and now life beyond time and space? Source was truly amazing, all-knowing, all-seeing. I told Source: "I can not stay with you. Your love is immense; your beauty is incomparable to anything I will ever know, but I have to go. I have to leave the dark. I can not yet quit my love for earth". I saw myself arise from the land of the non-physical into the physical plane through the thought of my earthbound heart.

I felt myself arise. Life beyond breath had been set into motion. I saw my heart become active. I saw that breath keeps life attached to my body, and a desire to love ignites the process. I saw that every breath with my earthbound body would be a gift. Every memory of earth is a wonder. Sharing my earthbound heart with my significant others would be an incomparable present of The All. That is why I came back to earth; even when I had a chance to leave. That is why I am running circles in this thing called life. That day I truly decided to live my life.

I died that day. How could man reappear in form after experiencing death? How could man escape the land of the non-psychical? How could man arise from a substance of what is seemingly all dark? How could spirit find humankind in a land so dark?

I died. I saw that. I accepted that. I left Into a time beyond the relative state of existence experienced through body and mind. I saw time set free of man-mind. I had left the earth. I saw myself being erased from All. I saw the void. I had finally become one; become All.

I had found the world's greatest treasure. Who did not want this? I had found the source of life, and I could not tell anyone. Why? I had to bring death upon them. What I want them to see is hidden behind their biggest fear; hidden beyond what all would die to protect; hidden beyond time and space; life and death; family and friends; success and love.

I knew that death would never come to anyone; but how could I tell them; how could I show them what lies beyond our lives? How could a citizen of the world possibly forgive themself knowing they willingly had died; killed themself in body-mind; willingly had left all behind? How could they value living knowing that death would never come? How could they continue knowing that life had no meaning; how could they overcome the ultimate sensation of freedom; how could they overcome the unforgettable blessing of The All in All?

The light said to me: "Did you think being free was easy? Do you think you can be free with the foundation of having a choice in this world? That is not freedom; it is a liberated version of free; it is being free of doubt, it has nothing to do with freedom. Being free of doubt is actually the opposite of being free. Who made you think freedom of choice has anything to do with freedom?"

The light continued: "Freedom requires no choice; it involves no liberation. It requires no action. It requires nothing. You are not free by making a choice or by having a choice. Do not pursue freedom. Do not wait for freedom. Freedom is to be touched by no-thing, not even by choice, chance, or time and space itself. Free is being free of All, and yet one with All."

The Light said to me: "Do you think you know what it means to be yourself? To understand what it means to take a stand and have an opinion; do as you please and serve nothing else than life itself? Do you believe in sailing the river of determination from within, connecting yourself to nothing else than nothing itself? Do you think you know what it means to reach beyond everything you see as reality?"

The light continued: "You seize to repeat what is already seized, and seize to repeat what is already perceived. Let me kill your belief to seize what is so easily deceived. Let me bleed into the streams and seas, and let your fleeing dreams be free. Be your own master and your own slave; be your own in every way; in every name."

The scariest part of exploring the universe is not seeing time and space and entities, it is seeing your friends and family and mind be torn apart. Everything comes with a price. See that everything you currently love, believe, and enjoy will be taken away. See what you currently believe to be real, burn to the ground. See reality arise from the ground of the dark. See life bound by the earth-bound boundaries arise from the dark.

People talk about their heritage; they talk about the importance of family. They talk about the significance of their blood and their collective mind. They all seem to have forgotten their origin, darkness, and light; feminine and masculine; him and her from within. They have forgotten their departure and arrival through The All. They got lost in the thought of All. You did not come from your parents. You came through your parents. You came from The All in All. You just came here through the portal of your earthborn mother, the mother and the son both share the light and the dark of The All.

The All in All was not bound by death, not bound by thought. Mind had created the universe through the belief in matter. Matter did not create this world. Mind was alone; I was alone. Matter had come to deceive the mind with love; as a child had come to blind its parents with love; as the divine had come to blind itself with its love for life.

That which is free of mind is free of death. Life exists beyond all time and space. Open your ancient eye. See your firstborn child. See the fire put into the eye of him and her. See the source, see The All in All. You came to fall in love in the eye of All. Free your mind and you will be free of death.

She was already born and still not here, she lived in no time but she was still alive. She told me: "I will stand after you by name, but never be after you." She appeared invisible and yet present; she had a vibrant form; all pure and undefinable. I could not perceive her complete nature; I could not make sense of her; I only saw a glimpse of her. I only saw a part of her available in myself; a part I came to call love.

Only The All can truly understand All, and only All can truly describe The All. One can only survive and be understood through the rule of two. Only through the rule of two can the universe perceive and be perceived. No one can perceive more than one can perceive oneself to be. That is how she hid in plain sight. She hides behind her own belief to perceive herself. Open your heart and your eyes will see yourself in her. Open your heart and she will be revealed in All.

Information at high speed is considered of high value and of truth. Don't get fooled by what can be moved. All can be moved; all elements of light and darkness, the dead and the living, all can be moved. High speed is not of higher truth. You, yourself, should understand this. Everything in the hands of everybody can easily be perceived as everything. Money, religion, war, light, racism, knowledge, friends; all in motion. By nature none of them are all good, all true, or all worthy. They are all in motion. All of the mind.

A single dollar; a single nationalist; a single song can appear infinite in nature with the right energy in motion. eMotion will give it size, mass, and subjective truth. It can fill an infinite mind-space, appear infinite true, and infinite big for a sleeper. This is the nature of subjective truth, eMotion. What is being moved is of eMotional value, mind-life. This is how subjective truth is evolved and put in motion and justified through relativity; you feel the truth, you feel what you, yourself, have put into motion; makes sense of; and gains value from.

Energy can not be destroyed; eMotion can not be put to rest through the mind, but the mind can be transcended. Money does not move, houses do not move, hate does not move, minds move. What is of value is of mind. What is moved; is moved by the mind. What is true, is of the mind. All are in mind. See the nature of the waves in everything. All come from the mind. All waves, all in mind.

What is low in motion is considered dead: See the human heart; rocks; the stock market. Mind is only that which is truly infinite in nature. Only in mind death exists. Mind projects truth; it projects itself. Mind projects motion. The mind can't be killed, the mind can be still, the mind can be put to rest. Put your mind to rest and you will find yourself beyond a life-time.

Do not believe and do not, not believe. Both are entertaining the mind; not elevating the mind. Do not think in terms of right and wrong; good or bad; positive and negative. Awake your mind. Simply see. Release the mind of seriousness; your illusionary involvement of mind; your incomprehensible desire to know through your mind. Let go of the mind; let the mind project its own desire and goals. Let your mind live; let your mind grow; let go of your mind-self. Let your attachment of mind go. Do not become attached to the mind.

Become silent; see that nature exists beyond your perception of the mind. See that mind can become still, see that mind can be transcended. See that right and wrong do not exist; only various desires of minds. See that mind runs on eMotion; see that mind is the conquer of worlds; see that mind runs on the desire to expand, to be all, yet separate from all, keeping the mind from All. Let go of your mind, draw your power from a state beyond your mind-life.

Can you hear the vibration beyond your mind? The call beyond your senses? Can you hear the flow of light that is constantly ready to shape the reality you call life? Can you hear the eternal flame? Can you see the eternal flicker; can you feel the eternal vibration; can you feel the electricity, the readiness of reality? Can you see that life only grows based on your ability to boost, see and embrace The All in All?

Your belief in putting your arm into motion is the same belief shaping tomorrow, and the same belief shaping matter through the mind. Nothing can grow in matter if it can not grow in mind. The truth lies in the enlargement of the mind. No religion can grow through numbers; only through altered states of mind. No-thing can be raised in numbers, only states of mind.

KNOW THIS MOMENT

What happens after death? I see it. I go back, I see, it changes. Death changes. What happens after tomorrow? Tomorrow changes. You keep coming back to the idea of tomorrow; you keep coming back to tomorrow through today, but tomorrow keeps changing in your mind; tomorrow will never come.

Ask yourself; what will happen here and now, and everything will be clear to you. Do you want to know death or be conclusive about death? People ask about death with certain assumptions, they ask about the future with certain assumptions; death and tomorrow are of the same nature yet perceived differently. Death is here; tomorrow is here. As your ignorance is seemingly infinite your opportunity to know will be the same. Simply see. Become open to The All. Know this moment, and you will know everything else. Take care of this moment and you will take care of everything; moment by moment.

What happens at the end of time? She will stand before you in the abyss. She will be your longing and forever lost love. You will stand in a void full of love with the bare minimum to experience time and space, and communicate a final statement: "I love". You will have experienced all love and sorrow, wars and pleasure. All-time on the inside-out.

You will stand with joy in your eyes and know that this is the last time you will see each other in a billion years. You will agree to forget; you will agree to shatter yourself into pieces and spread across all of existence. Create life together. Fall in love. Depart and arrive. You will forget so that you one day can remember.

One day you will wake up. You will see her in everything. You will see that your love never left you. You were never separated from the love you felt in your heart. Your long-lost love was here all along. She was hiding in your ability to love. You are where you belong. Your love was here all along.

When you isolate expansion from memory; experience expansion without memory, the world is yours. The big bang theory is complete. If you drop your idea of what is, you will make space for the truth. Remember where you are. You are of The All.

An altered mind will become man's most powerful instrument. Your eyes are not seeing the light; you are light. You don't hear the sound; you are sound. You will see this. You will explore this and feel free; you will see you are not limited to light speed and information in motion. You can speak to beings living before the great before, beings with no start or end, no limitations to your understanding of time. These beings can tell stories before times of the light and the time in space. You will remember their stories because they will tell stories about You.

It all started with a word, Adam is the first man of this world; a world built for Eve. He spoke, and we can see his word echoing through creation; he gave everything a name, in her name. Everything is waves; everything is the spoken words of Adam and Eve.

The masculine builds life, but the feminine makes life worth living. I will create a paradise; I will keep you safe, Eve. I can not leave without you; I can not do it without you. My separate sense of self; my eyes on her; my love for her keeps my heart attached to the earth.

EMBRACE YOUR SEXUALITY

You may feel suppressed or robbed by your sexuality but know it all comes from within. All comes from the seed of your sexuality and energy to give and create. Do not feel ashamed to let your energy into this world, and do not feel embarrassed to bring down the barriers built around those who are not yet able to see. Free the spirit of sexual suppression. Free the light in your heart. Free your sexuality and be potent towards the world.

Out of the darkness came two doors, two doors were opened. One door was mechanical. I had to open the door with brute strength; with the force of my heart. With no dedication, focus, and determination the door would stay locked before me. I could only see what was behind the first door of heaven by putting will and power into life.

The second door was organic. I could only open the door through openness; by surrendering. The door was already open. My desire to open the door would keep it closed. I had to let go. I was already on the inside and the outside of the door. I had to trust, I had to surrender to love. I had to fall through the door of my inner world. I could only see what life had for me through vulnerability, trust, and surrender.

I ask the Lord: "Who am I? How did I get here? What is a human? Show me." The Lord said to me: "Are you sure?" I told the Lord: "Yes". The two doors of heaven were opened before me. I was tested before entering the realm of sacred knowledge. Before the doors arose a light so pure that I felt like dying, burning up. I was hit with such pure information that the lies I had built my life upon fell to the ground. I felt great pain. I immediately removed myself from the light.

The first thing the Lord told me was: "You already know. You have simply forgotten. You have built this place; You have put yourself here." Light and love fell upon my soul like a tsunami of fire purifying my being. I died. Everything was completely dark; a sacred space, like no space, delimited by walls, pure dark mass became alive. Potent and steady. From the pure space, I saw a force running circles around two creatures. The two creatures were not complete, they were of energy, molded and raised from the dark; made from a pure and silent substance. I can only describe it as living energy.

The Lord said to me from the dark: "It's all about experiencing the human being, being in life, enjoying yourself. You can always get out of the experience if you do not want to be here anymore. It creates space for others. Do you want to leave?" and I answered: "No" The Lord said: "Why?" and I answered: "Because I want to love. I want to be here as a human being".

My guide said to me: "Trust that everything will work out perfectly fine; enjoy how amazing your creation is. Say yes to life, listen to life, trust your life and give your love, trust, and gratitude to all your being. Let life's pleasant surprises come to you and let them come to others. You have sent yourself here and only you know why. You are wonderful, remember to help everyone realize they are the same."

My guide continued: "The world is full of love, see it, fall in love and let love flow into every plane of reality. Let it flow and one day you will stand with tears in your eyes; joy incomparable to anything you have ever seen; a heart full of love and a life full of gratitude. Go out and live your life and remember where you come from, see me with you wherever you go."

This world is of a chaotic order for your language and words. You are told to believe that what you understand is explainable, but higher realms are not measured in your pronunciation or ability to speak. Your voice and your words are a fragment of The All.

Do not think The All could fit into anybody's ears or be expressed by anybody's tongue. You are possessing tools to make sense beyond the mind; sense far beyond what comes as voice or words. Worlds beyond the sine. How would one speak a star? How could one speak life? How would one speak what gives words creational power? Open your heart to the magic of your being. Know beyond your ability to listen and to speak. Know beyond what can be explained or understood. Know worlds beyond the world of spelling; know beyond the world of belief.

There is an order to all, a significance to all elements. Understand this order, explore the four languages of life, then you will see space open her eternal library to you. It is the job of an alchemist to understand and purify all aspects of water, air, earth, and fire, to open one's heart-space. Remove all the fog from man's heart. Fire is the element most important to the alchemist; all the alchemist does is purify the heart and mind through cycles.

See that heat shapes all things. You are shaped in the eternal flames of life. See how heat appears. Your fire will be your eternal truth. If your electric reality becomes illusory, look for fire. Feel the fire. Anything can be transformed in the eternal flame; anything can be altered within you. You will see everything be forged in the eternal fire. Where you see heat, you will be happening. Where there is fire, there is You.

PURE LIGHT

Pure light appeared to me in a dream; I traveled with light. I saw geometries being shaped in the presence of this light, I saw all things, all life grow from the involvement of geometry. The order of light, the laws of light, the intention of creation, and the desire to love beyond all.

I saw the evolution of information, I saw the birth of love. I saw the comings and goings of the light. I saw the organic be taken over by the mechanical; I saw the conscious move into the unconscious. I saw destruction before creation, the process of change in life's cycles.

The Lord of the dark said to me: "There is a layer beyond memory, a key to changing your reality. Like your mindset can change your reality, new layers of mind can change matter. See, there are the circles of memory, your life, and then there are the circles and lectures of intelligence. People, be aware of these and see the difference."

The Lord of the dark continued: "These are circles of your being, chosen and put into motion by yourself. See, you have memories exceeding the day. These things are called evolution or growth; it is what you call consciousness, becoming aware of your being; these small glimpses of reality, breaking the patterns of your camouflage. Do you see? Wake up from the dream you call yourself."

What is the nature of Ego? There are different levels of consciousness, streams of thought, layers of reality. You can become available and exposed to power beyond comprehension. You can bring light to yourself. Access realms layered like the atmospheres of the earth.

Ego is the bottle cap of the creational self, a force separating your containment of sensation from the absolute truth of The All. Protecting your being from accurate and direct hits from The Dweller in the dark. Ego is a force withholding your ordered self from seemingly chaotic worlds. Do not force your ego open in times of weakness, carry your Ego with love into this life and the next.

Be grateful for the atmosphere of Ego; layers of Ego; be aware of the development of Ego; be thankful for the containment of self; the maturation of self. Be open for the opportunity of altered states, be open towards worlds kept hidden behind layers of self-preservation; layers of Ego-death; layers of the sensation of self.

You want to know the nature of enlightenment; the language of light; the ancient tongue, speaking across all time and space. You want to obtain the state of a self-taught god; the enlightened one. You want to know what lies behind the intellect of your mind. You want to transcend what you always thought to be real.

Seek and you will find. The world around you is not what it seems. It is filled with mysticism; it is filled with subtle vibrations; filled with Truth of The All. Information kept and preserved for those worthy of The All. Truth living undetected and yet visible to All. Open your heart and your tongue will align. Open your heart and you will speak the language of light.

ACCEPTANCE OF THE DARK

You will know all of humanity if you can understand the realm of darkness and accept its nature and validity. Accept the darkness in man, and God will accept the darkness in you. You are blinded or hurt by that which is not accepted within yourself. Accept, and life will be yours. You can accept all of yourself when you can accept all in others.

You can mirror yourself in the light, but can you see yourself in the darkness of The All? To understand why people hurt and love, and accept hurt and love as equals; see that you contain the seed of both the light and the dark. See that both truth and lies; in and out; good and evil are of The All. There is no evil, simply degrees of goodness; nothing is done in evil but at times of relatively small degrees of goodness. Understand that all are done in some good. Understand that All is of The All. Accept to become one with All.

I spoke: "Lord of the dark; I have been blessed with memories of your presence; I have told my long-lost love stories of your being; I have brought to my long-lost love and myself the greatest of All: The blessing of your love; the highest of causes. How can I still not feel love for myself or attract my long-lost love?"

The Lord of the dark spoke: "You came to me asking; "I am good enough?". To hear it from me, and now that you hear it, you still feel lost. You need to see that acceptance only matters when it comes from your own being. There is no hierarchy or percentage of acceptance; there is only your own acceptance; the worth that you hear and see for yourself. You came to me to confirm your worth, but you now see that nobody can accept you except yourself. Your worth can come from nowhere else than within; it can come from nowhere else than yourself."

Do not favor others, dead things, or beliefs. Be in favor of that which lives in creativity, love, and divinity. The story in all tales. Be in favor of your feelings transcending logic; be in service of yourself; see within yourself, what you are and what you wish to be. Put your eye into a telescope and you will see the stars. Put your heart into your dreams and unimaginable growth stands before you.

Parts of your being are waiting to be unfolded. Life comes down to nothing more than an unfolding of self. Simply be and you will naturally grow through space and time. Spend time and energy on what you love; spend time on yourself, and you will grow. Put your heart into life; become a co-creator of your reality. Be consistent with the things you love and see them grow.

It is a myth that you will never get back time. You are time. You never had any time and will never get any time. Time is what you are. See time all around you. When did you become separate from time? Clock-time is a creation of the mind. Neither does it run and neither does it stand. You did not come into time, you came out of time. Everything comes from everything; The All in All and All in The All.

What you call time is simply a list of desires; a wish towards your existence. A man living in the desert, doing nothing, is of less time than a person with a tight schedule, running the streets of New York. Neither will run out of time. They are the foam of time; a consequence of time; a temporary bubble from time encountering vast space. You will go back in time as a wave goes back into the ocean. Whatever time you came with is what you desire. What you are given is the time it takes. What you live is truly what you want. Time can neither come nor go. Time is what you are.

The Dark Lord spoke to me: "From that world, your ideas arise, you will once again arrive and arise. It is not death. Do you see death before creation; or do you see love; do you see life? Death is only limited to the limitations of your appreciation and understanding of your being. What is not expressed will dwell in the deep dream, but can anytime be taken into The All. We all come from the body of the mountain but live as separates yet to become as one through creation."

The Dark Lord Continued: "See that everything of this world is of belief. If you lose your faith you lose your world. The world is of your own making. All is of your own making. All that is true is of you. What is real is what you choose to believe. See that nothing exceeds the importance of your own desire to become and to love."

The Lord spoke to me: "It is not in your nature to fear but act in love. Life may resist, but it can never destroy. In times of fear, see you are in the dark. Step into the light; light will come to you in mysterious ways".

"When you become free of fear; when you accept uncertainty; when you let death into your heart the world will be yours. Only fear lives in the mortal's dream. Be a warrior. Be courageous. Fear is only resistance in your being. Let go. Let fear arise from even the darkest halls in your being. Face your fears and see yourself become one with All".

"Only a heart with no fear can enter heaven; only with a light heart can one open the eye of The All. Only with no directional pull can one escape the idea of All. Your heart has to be united through love and trust to become one with All. Let go of the weight of your earthbound thoughts; let go of all fear or your separation from The All".

Heaven spoke to me: "You are not ready to see beyond the color of your skin, religion, and culture of your earthborn family. You only see half the truth cause you live as half your being. You are right about racism but only half right, and only when you see the face of your brothers transcending all senses, then you will be ready to regain power. Until that day, you will slowly grow into awareness, not yet grow into your highest being. You think you know the face of racism, but you will be ready to know when you truly see."

The Enlightened one spoke to me: "You have been told stories of the last prophet, but this world will never run out of prophets or the need for enlightened beings. Remember, no-thing can hide in the light unless you have been blinding your mind's eye".

"The truth will never deny the seeker; only the seeker can deny the truth. Open your mind's eye to the light of All; dare to reach for the scepter of The All. Dare to take the power to unite All. Go into the eternal flame with no fear; go into the fire with a heart full of love; sacrifice All to become reborn with a scepter to lead All. Go with an empty mind and all will be yours. Become pure of heart and the strength of The All will be yours".

The Enlightened one said to me: "The scepter gives the one worthy of its power, light, and love, in the time needed to do good in this world. A king is not born from a human bloodline nor is a leader of the world elected by the people. A king and true leader of All are given the light of the gods to do good here and now; do what they have set their heart to do with unconditional -and unselfish love. Power is not given by proving oneself worthy in the eyes of others; power does not exist in the eyes of others; power exists in your heart; by proving oneself worthy to do good in the eyes of the gods. Only through sacrifice; only through unselfish acts of love; only through the death of self can the scepter become yours".

"The power of the king's scepter does not come from memory; it can not rule through the memory of self; it can not be yielded beyond now; it can not be contained or kept for oneself. The scepter is only given in times of presence and love. Become conscious of now and the scepter will be yours".

Creation said to me: "Know Thy curves placed in the center of Thy palms. Know Thy power to see lay before Thy. See, Thy palms are Thy keys to arise All into creation. See, All is born from the dwelling symphony placed at the core of every palm. Open Thy world by opening Thy palms. Look from left to right. Look into the space of Thy palms. Open Thy heart by opening Thy palms. Know Thy power lies before Thy. Know Thy breath through the mold of Thy Palms. Know Thy power through Thy Palms"

"Who are you?" she said. Time told her: "As our paths met today, they will part again. Our day becomes night and our night becomes day, I am just a visitor of night and day, a visitor to this office and a visitor of this world. Where the sea and the sky meet in the horizon I stand hidden before your eyes."

"In a few years my visit on earth will be over and I will again take off from here. I am a visitor to the earth as I am a visitor to you. As I am given food at a restaurant I am given a body on earth. All a part of the experience. It is a process of understanding oneself. To mirror oneself in the crystal of time. Get closer to oneself through life. I am a being of The All camouflaged with the face of a life-time".

Heaven spoke to me: "Do not call upon dark forces to prove yourself. Do not cast magick that you can not recall. Keep yourself in the light. A man wanted to prove the existence of demons to his neighbor standing with his daughter and wife. The man wanted to prove himself to his ignorant neighbor. The pride of the man poisoned his heart. The man's need to prove himself to his ignorant neighbor gave life to dark thoughts."

"The man called death upon them all. The man called hell upon earth. The man had let the poison created by his heart into the world. The man released a sickness into the world. The man immediately saw what he had done, but it was too late. The man had created an evil, he, himself could not stop. The man saw the devil mirrored back to me in the face of his neighbor. The man failed the test. The pride of the man destroyed them all; the man found himself lost. The man's need to be right had brought a little more hell on earth."

"Be conscious of the spells you cast upon the earth. Act in love and not in pride. Open the gates of heaven and not the gates of hell. Both can be opened. What will come to you is what you chose to bring into this world. What you chose to make of the world, the world will become."

The light talked to me: "Open your mind's eye, my child. Great evil may remain hidden in the eyes of the earthborn but can easily be seen in the light. Through light, a secret order will be revealed to you. It is time to awake your sleeping soul. They may remain a minority to stay in the shadows; speak as if they are victims of a primitive cause, but they are not. Know Thy that we see; know Thy that we do not believe; know Thy that we will build on top of Thy."

I asked the void, "What is life about?" The void said to me with its calm voice: "It's about perspective". The void shot an echo through time cycling around my being, a cycle of time, I felt like the center of a clock. Always in the same position but always perceiving the day from a new angle; untouched in time but always in a position to receive impressions of the time-cycle.

THE GUARD

I met a being while walking in the park, a being that presented itself as a Guard. This creature was the Guard between heaven and earth, the Watcher of earth, and the Guard wanted to teach me how to access heaven.

This Guard said to me: "I have no family, I do not eat, I do not live on earth, I do not have a food-body, but I am here. What you see as others I see as myself. What you see as there I see as here. What you see as yourself I see as part of myself. I can help you evolve your mind; I can help you understand new dimensions of life. I can show you the pathway to the next life; an altered state of mind."

The Guard said to me: "I will help you understand and integrate your light and your love. I will show you how to step in and out of the gateway of heaven. I will teach you, so you one day may become a protector of the light"

The Guard continued: "Right now heaven is of the mind to you. You fear your own light. Escape your mind and heaven will be yours. The light of your mind can be seen as the wall of your life. Life beyond mind, life beyond the walls of mind can be yours. The mind keeps you from seeing yourself; see beyond the mirror on your wall-mind. See yourself mirrored in The All. The mind is the protector of worlds; the mind keeps you from falling in a hell loop, but it also keeps you from spiraling into heaven".

"Let the first lessons to you be this: let go of the fear of starving. Let go of what you see as the most important and essential element in your life. What separates beings of light and humans of the earth is the fear of dying, the element of survival, their attachment to their food-body, and survival-mind. You have to transcend the primitive instinct of survival. See that food is fine, see that reproduction is fine, but do not become attached to the life of a beast. Few men live beyond the dimension of survival. They are simple primates running a complex cycle to get feed and reproduce. Do not let survival poison your heart. See what life will bring through courageous acts of love instead of constant acts to survive."

The watcher said: "As you carry a mission in your heart, so do the angels of heaven. We have our own life and evolve through time. Let me show you life from the perspective of my eye". Life became so intense that I could take a non-locative perspective; experience higher time. I was with the angels in the realm of One. A perspective of seemingly organized chaos. A liquid version of mind. What I previously experienced as solid in the material world had become light in a world of belief.

A had become one with the air. The one thing the watcher told me before I escaped my mind was: "Feel the wind against your skin". My skin disappeared. The wind went through me and there was no air running in and out of my lungs. I was weightless. There was no breathing. There was just the air going through me, nothing in front and behind me. I was here, but I did not feel alive. I felt like a genie leaving its bottle through the touch of an angel on my body. The watcher said: "You now see, there are no people standing in front or behind of me. Everything that you believe to arise from chaos is organized through my mind. Nothing stands in the way of each other, hates each other, or loves each other. The whole thing is one combined thought. This is the perspective of a halo-mind. As an angel, you lose yourself to the love for man. Like man, lose itself to the love for thought. You nurture certain thoughts as we nurture certain people. Thoughts can as well as people become conscious and alive. I live in this light, above, yet here with you as a mere perspective of The All."

An angel with a name introduced himself to me, an angel of historical significance to the east. An angel that let the light come to the one singing the one song. An angel with a halo exceeding the street; an angel with light present in All. The light of a higher realm; light with the intensity to power a collective body of potentially All.

The angel is of the archangels. The angel spoke to me of the prophet: "The prophet came to me. The prophet came to me with true intention. The prophet was a good man, pure of heart; the prophet came to me asking for a family above all. I promised the prophet one above all; a family greater than all others".

The archangel said: "A prophet is a receiver of the light; A prophet is an arch carrying the weight of an angel, allowing the light of heaven to pass onto him and the people of the earth. See that the prophet is only a door kept open for people to mirror themselves in The All; the mirror of possibility. The prophet is simply man no more. The prophet has given up All to be a servant of The All.

The archangel continued: "I will show the process of a prophet. I will show the world building on the light of an archangel. I will show you the meaning of the crown." The archangel showed me heaven. The hierarchy of angels, the workings of the light. The strength and overwhelming power of truth. The archangel said to me: "As layers of the earth protect your body from the light of the sun. We, the angels, protect your being from the light of The All. We are no gods, only servants of The All. We are simply layers built to serve above all".

The mind said to me: "See the mind as you see the world. There are worlds beyond the world you know, the world you call home, the brain, here, yourself. There are versions of self transcending your sense and thought of self; your physical self. One who only thinks with one's eyes is blind to the possibility of The All. One who only thinks from the thought of self is blind to multiple selves. You have to see that the brain is only a part of the mind available to a surgeon. Awake the whole mind. Awake the multi-dimensional mind."

The mind continued: "How can one access the mind, beyond the brain? There is a new mind wandering the dark; still in the dark; a mind yet to ignite; a mind with abilities far beyond your logical bandwidth. Expand the mind. One can travel the universe through consciousness with the right mind. The right mind can entertain several lives. One can travel space without a spacecraft. There is no distance with the right mind in space and time. Become open to the possibility of the multi-dimensional mind".

Of all the stories I can tell of heaven, altered states of mind, otherworldly beings, planes of reality; of all things I know, one story exceeds them all. The story of the one I Love. The story of her. The her to my him. The one thing people want to know; the one thing I never get tired of thinking of. I never speak of her by name. I only speak of the meaning she has to me.

How do I know it is her? Because it is simple. I know her. I know her as I know myself. I remember her as I remember myself. I know her by the feeling of her skin like I know myself by the feeling of my own skin. I know the sweetness of her touch and the love of her heart. I know because I desire no other. I know because I love no other.

Time might have torn us apart; life may have brought us our separate ways. But my love for her never faded; my love for her is never complicated. My feelings for her are true. Her love is the only real thing I have encountered in a world of constant change; comings and goings. She transcends the day and the night; the earth and the sky. She lives beyond all time. Beyond all sense of my earthborn body and beyond all ideas put into motion by my mind.

Even though we talk no more, simply living with the possibility of meeting her; having the chance to stand up for her; having a body to carry her in my heart, makes life worth living. Even the face of the gods can not compare to the beauty of her touch; the beauty of her face; her voice and what she expresses. I will always be thankful to The All for bringing me such joy and love. I will always be thankful to The All for bringing me to her.

I spoke to the void; "I miss her so much. What should I do to get her back?" The void said to me: "You need to take control of yourself. Because she is what you are". And I said: "What is she?". The void told me: "She is everything" I said: "Yeah, she is everything to me. I would like to make her happy, I would like to do something special for her".

The void said: "You have been shown the nature of duality, but you do not understand duality to the full extent. See that she is everything and everything is what you are; she and everything she is you are. See the oneness of All, become whole, only in this way can your love grow. Only in this way will you know. You have to be everything for yourself, to be everything for her. She is your anger, sorrow, joy, and truth as you are hers. Become whole, become all that. Accept her through yourself. All you deal with is of her being, and all she deals with is of your being. Live as one and you will know."

The void said to me: "I see that you tell yourself that she doesn't love you anymore and that she never did love you. We both know it is not true. You have become impossible to love. You have become bitter with the feeling of her being gone. You have poisoned your mind. You got lost in the time and space of your mind. You have forgotten what is important. You have destroyed your mind and what it contains. Let go. You have to remember what is important. Your mind and your memories are a gift. Let go of past."

The void continued: "You have consumed yourself; forgot the origin of the past. You have been taught not to forget; you have been schooled and given a lot to remember through life. But you forgot to remember what to forget and forgot what to remember. You forgot what the past is here for. You are not the past. It's not the source of your power, it's not your source of intelligence. The past is not the foundation of love. The past was given to you to remember what is worth remembering. Remember to remember what is important; remember what is most important to you, create that world; pursue that world. Show her your love, show her here and now."

The void said: "Your problem is not that you are alone in the dark. You are alone; you are in the dark. Your problem is that you think you're the only one alone in the dark. Look around you; you are alone in the dark, but so is everyone else. She was alone in the dark and you were not there for her. You have been busy feeling sorry for yourself, even with all the light you were given."

The void continued: "It never occurred to you to check on her. It never occurred to you what she might have felt. You were not there for her, but trust what your heart sees. You know she still cares about you, but a lot has happened. Be open to her, nothing less and nothing more. It is so simple. Be open and available. Look at her and you will know. See her for who she is and she will come. Take control of yourself. She never asked anything of you, nothing of you but love for yourself."

I asked the void about a recurring dream: "I meet my long-lost love in different locations, we bump into each other and we agree to get lost. But in every scenario there is an event drawing my attention; I have to pick up a bike; I have to go for a quick walk; always something seemingly innocent. When I pull my attention towards her, again, she is gone. I can not sense her presence anymore. It is like all-time in the world has gone by and I just stand there without her, lost, out of time."

The void said to me: "Do not forget what you ultimately carry in your heart through life. You remember her. I can see it, but you're still not focused. You're losing your way. You´re still letting yourself be interrupted by the outside world. Know yourself to overcome the noise. You are the only one lost, no one else. Only by finding yourself will you get to her. Let go of your senses and listen to your heart. Let go of the world. Sit down and find peace. Find peace within yourself and peace will spread to everything around you. You will be the master at all times. Be aware of your attention and determination; be aware of your heart; become alive through the things you choose to love and live by".

I had a dream: "I saw tomorrow and yesterday, deja vu and recognition; a restart of things in mind. There were two forms of yesterday; one came from oblivion; the other came from memory. Some things have repetition and others do not. Something new is added as something else is extracted. Something is added and simultaneously removed; taken from one place to another."

"There was a cycle. There was a world of fantasy and a world of memories. Life had two directions. The distribution of space-time can be seen as the consumption of events, like the consumption of products; it is the optimization of space-time; to do everything efficiently; to place everything where it should be; to get the moments of time distributed across life."

I saw the universe arise, here. Right now. The big bang happens all the time; arising through a false vacuum. Life is folded around a membrane, like air in a lung; a sphere curled around an element. Bubbles that inflate, emerged, and constantly disappeared in and out of nowhere/now-here. The brain builds realities through this quantum mechanical process. Everything breathes. Everything are bubbles; bubbles forming portals by intersecting; forming the world you know, the way of life.

I traveled through worlds; I traveled through portals, intersections of universes. I reached a plane containing nine creatures of light. They looked at each other and said: "He can see us". All nine beings looked at me, they had no mouth, they were all 180 cm tall, and were built of pure light. They did not present themselves as angels, but beings of light. They did not speak and I did not hear. We communicated, telepathically. I knew their thoughts, thoughts they made available to me. I could not read their minds; we were simply communicating with no use of the mouth, only the mind.

I always wondered how intelligent life on other planets would look like. I never thought I would find it on earth. Find it here. I saw that earth is populated by otherworldly beings. I have come into mental contact with the light before, but this was the first time I saw beings of light before my eyes.

I flew past the plane containing creatures of light. I reached the speed of light; a dimension with no time or space; everything stood still; an endless loop, the same thing stopped and started in the same space. I realized that everything had come to an end. The light had stopped; the realm of time in motion had stopped. The light stood before me. Simply constant in life. The snake had bid its own tail. The creator and creation had reached the same vibration; an equivalent state in space-time.

I could feel the weight of the sun's rays as I could feel the wind on my body; as if the light had been frozen, physical. Time simply stopped. But still, I was free. Know, you can not shoot yourself free from the light through the laws of light. You are pure light shot through the mind. What you see as light and call as life is only a bending of The All; cold light.

You will encounter the outermost layer of the bubble; you will experience the wall of the light, right here. You can take your head out of the light with the right mind. You will see the one thing faster than light. The one thing more significant than what moves; what travels. Mind did not stop at light speed. Mind was untouched by space-time. I still had thoughts and feelings; an experience. I am not defined by light, light is defined by the mind; time is defined by the mind.

I have seen all the light of the sun. I have seen the sun burn out. I have walked the surface of the mind-life of sun-light; the body of earth's sun. I have seen the end of time for the earth's sun-light. I have escaped the star of the night. I have become a star free of the night. I came to a land with a star born through the dark mass; a mass full of light yet seemingly all dark.

You are living as a mass with an uneven equivalent to the sun's light. You are living with an uneven equivalent to the mind. You carry a weight relative to your environment; relative to the unconscious state of mind. You are living in the cold light. You are living in between the charge of worlds; the charge of mind bringing gravity into life. You are of mass in the sun's light. The mass of a sun-mind. Gravity goes far deeper than just mass from an object. Gravity exists in the mind. Gravity moves on several planes. Gravity is alive in states of mind.

I asked the Dark Lord: "How can man travel through the darkness in the future? How can civilization arrive in this next world of the dark star" The Dark Lord said to me: "See that you are born through the same air as the one around you; arise from the same earth that holds all structures of nature; and are powered through the same fire as All."

"You stand before the same laws that bring life to the waves at sea and the wind in the air. I taught you how to sail the sea without a single location, you knew nothing of arrival or achieving, only exploring. See that you need to explore and set sail in the dark to sail time and space as you do the seas. It is like no places you know of today, the map will be set in dark-time, but till then you simply have to see. When you know how to sail the ocean of darkness you have come far".

THE BECOMING OF THOUGHT

I asked the Lord of All: "Can you show me the becoming of All? Can you show me the way of thought and how it arises?" The Lord of All said: "Empty your mind and see life arise from the silence". My mind became silent and life exploded. Life arose from thought. Emotions and thoughts became alive. All I wanted I thought, all I thought I wanted. Thought arose from the dark with such intent; with such tremendous force. There was no stopping thought. There was no stopping my gift to have what I wanted. My free will; my power of thought. By simply wanting, there was thought, and through thought, I had what I wanted.

The Lord of All said: "Get in touch with what you want. Get in control of your thoughts. Know that this life can be yours". By not knowing what I want chaos arose from thought. By fearing what I saw, darkness arose from thought. By trying to escape what I was, separation arose from thought. I became afraid of the power of thought. I became conscious of thought and I became conscious of what I wanted. I started to see that out of the chaos came order, out of the darkness came light, out of fear came courage. I saw a natural order to life. A natural order of thought and how it all came from what I want. I simply sat, became aware of thought, now knowing that I could have all I want through thought.

I had this dream: "My family and friends stand before my body; my body is getting crucified, I hang on a cross. They are all laughing. I remember looking down from the cross feeling sorry for them all. They are mocking my cause. They are laughing at the thorns they will have to wear to be pronounced kings and queens of the heavens. They are laughing because it is easy, but I only wonder if they will dare to open their eyes in time to become one with The All".

There was a lesson in the experience; in my crucifixion. I heard it spoken with love. Love showed me that: "The deep wounds caused by the thorns were made in love; my wounds brought me closer to God. There was no difference between suffering and love. I experienced the tremendous pain as the nails went through my hands as the greatest love I had ever felt; it was all love; boundless love; an ascension. Love was not given or felt; love was everywhere I felt. Love was in everything. I could not escape God's love. There was no limit to how deep the pain felt and no limit to the depth of the love of The All. The harder they hit the nails into my hands, the deeper the pain felt, the closer I felt to God; till the only thing I could see was the love of The All. I arose from the cross and spiraled into a world of pure love."

Do you know what I love about death? It consumes everything I am without warning. It takes everything I have and ever will be. It leaves me with no-thing. I can give all I am back, simply release my being with no other judgment than the one I put upon myself. Simply give in to the dweller and join the dark. Become one with The All.

When you fear death you no longer have anything to fear about death. You have become fearful of life itself. You have become separate from life itself. You can come no further away from the truth than knowing life through fear. It's time to open your heart. It is time to go live your life. Fear is an opportunity to live, learn and grow. Know that fear is simply the self-containment of that which we all share, a fear to let go of love and light. A desire to keep love and light for the idea of oneself; always keeping oneself separate from love and light. Let go. Death will come to all. See that death lives in all and gives life to all. See that death is of The All. See that love and light are spread by letting go of self-preservation.

I asked the lord of light: "I am dead?" The lord of light said to me: "You are not dead. You are in a relative state. You are dead to others but not to yourself. Your body is still intact. It is up to you if you want to return to your body; your life on earth or go into the light. To enter the light you have to empty your heart. Let go of your earthbound life, cast your heart into the oldest of fire; burn your love for life. You are in a state of dis-attachment, you have lost all belief, still, you are bound by your love for the mind. You are bound to the love of your earthbound heart. Love that can not enter heaven. Love that weighs on your unbound heart".

I got scared. I could hear the wings of an angel coming to bring me into the light; into the next life. I said to the Lord of the light: "Sorry that I doubted, sorry". I apologized with all of my heart. The lord of light said to me: "Go to your body and get up". I said: "But I can not see, I am lost. How can I still believe after all I have seen? How can I continue to live in this earthbound body? How can I unite with my body?". The lord of light said to me: "Look up. Take your head off the ground. Become alive." I opened my heart and there it was, my life. I have yet again returned to my earthbound life. All came back; sound, sight, heart, mind, body came alive. I had all my memories and expectations again; I was once again earthbound by heart.

The light said to Man: "If Man does not judge the light; if Man does not believe the light, does not, not believe the light. If Man does not live in the sea of I "am better than him", the sea of "he is stupid and I am clever" or the sea of "I am good and my neighbor is bad". If Man does not poison the sea of light. If Man simply sees the light with no judgment. If Man simply sees the one light, the ocean of blissful love. If Man sees the light, Man will rise.

The light continued: "Man-mind is an expert at making a drama of the light, the same light present in all minds, the same ray of sunlight, the same life. Man can make a hell out of the light or make a heaven of the light. Simply see the light is pure. The light needs no judgment of your mind. The light needs neither your positivity nor your guidance. If no judgment falls on the light, Man will rise. If Man empties their mind, the light will rise.

I remembered it all. I remembered life before I arrived on earth. Life beyond a life lived. How energy circulates. How thoughts arise. What life in heaven is like. Source played all reality before my eyes. All the life I chose; all the decisions I made. My journey towards the light. My life on Earth. All comings and goings of my life. All my joy and sorrow; love and hurt. I saw myself in All.

I chose this life. I saw myself moment by moment. I saw myself arrive at this exact moment. All I had ever done had put me here and now. I had chosen this life and I wanted to be nowhere else than here, right now. I saw what it meant to be human. To be human means: know that you chose it. When you know; when you accept; when you see, this is your life; your choice, then you will live as a human on Earth.

Remember my child, my knowledge is always available to you; my love can always be found in your heart. All I am given is also for you to see. What can I teach that you do not already know? Let the planes of reality taught to me enter your heart and separate yourself from your body. See there is no difference between you and I. Do not grief when we are no longer seen together in the visible light. Do not feel separated from me in my passing, see that all I am is now passing on to you.

Know that the same love given to me by the cosmos is present in you. Know that we are shapeshifters by nature and creators by heart. Know this life and you will know everything else. Know yourself and life will be yours. Step into the light and become one with The All. Put your heart into your life and become an inspiration to humanity. Join your brothers and sisters of the light. Know Thyself beyond space and time, look up into the sky, become a star free of the night. Become alive; Moment by Moment.